T0122135

To my son Isaac

In a small town in the Sawtooth Mountains lived a girl named Charlie, who was in the third grade.

Her real name was Charlotte, but that was too proper for a girl who didn't like wearing dresses or getting her hair combed.

She was a strong girl who liked to catch frogs and play with bugs. Her sisters and brother called her stubborn, but Charlie knew herself as determined.

Charlie's house lay between a creek and the Big Wood River. When she wasn't playing with her sisters and brother, Charlie liked to play along the bank of the creek near a little wooden bridge. Every spring, the snow melted off the Sawtooth Mountains, ran into the Big Wood River, and spilled over into the dry creek bed. The grasses along the banks flushed out into every shade of green: yellow greens, blue greens, and purple greens.

Charlie's favorites were the tall snake grasses. She liked to pull the segments apart and snap them back together. In summer, the creek was teeming with grasshoppers, ladybugs, and water skippers. Songbirds flew down from the towering cottonwood trees to drink, and the shimmering colors of the rainbow trout sparkled in the clear water. At summer's end, the creek dried up and was once again quiet for winter.

One late summer morning, barefoot as usual, Charlie waded into what was left of the creek, a small pool of muddy water. She hunched over and looked for the elusive rainbow trout that had escaped her the day before. Every year Charlie caught the rainbow trout that were trapped under the bridge and returned them to the Big Wood River before the creek dried up.

Charlie had caught all the fish except one, and she was determined to save the last rainbow trout! She rolled up her sleeves and slowly moved her hands in the muddy water. The thick mud squeezed through her toes, and every time she felt something move across her feet, she thought of the little spider bugs that lived in the water. It made her squirm, but she was not giving up.

Charlie kept searching, and then she felt the tail of the fish brush up against the back of her leg. She spun around and got a hold on him, but the slippery trout muscled his way out of her grasp.

The real trick, Charlie remembered, was to use her shirt to catch the rainbow trout. She held out the bottom of her shirt as far as it would stretch and searched through the water. She saw the water ripple between some branches and knew he must be hiding there. She moved in slowly and tried to corner the rainbow trout, but he escaped again.

She turned around and held her shirt out. She saw the tip of his tail come out of the water and darted in his direction. Suddenly, there he was, thrashing in her shirt! She closed the shirt around him and held the fish against her pounding heart.

She carefully carried him to the bucket. Splash! She had done it! The last rainbow trout was now safe and slowly circling in the bucket. Charlie smiled and took no notice that she was covered from head to toe with mud.

Charlie carried the heavy bucket down to the Big Wood River. With every step, a little splash of water jumped out of the bucket, leaving a trail of muddy water behind. She crossed the Big Wood River bridge and headed for a tall cottonwood tree that marked an opening in the fence where she could get through.

She passed through the fence and walked down to the foot of
Sawtooth Mountains, where the river ran deep and calm. She stood
at the water's edge. She liked to listen to the soft, steady rumbling of
the river and feel the cool breeze on her cheeks.

Charlie sat down and looked at the fish circling in the muddy water. It had been so hard to catch him that she was now reluctant to let him go. Still, she knew it was the right thing to do. As the beautiful trout circled in the bucket, Charlie talked to the fish. "I'm going to miss you," she whispered as tears ran down her cheeks, "but I know that you will be happy in the river!"

She listened to her heart, and she knew it was time to let the rainbow trout go. She lowered the bucket gently into the water. The clear, clean water mixed with the muddy water, and the trout swam over the edge of the bucket, down into the deep waters, and then out of sight.

Charlie set the bucket down and knelt by the river's edge. *If I could only see the beautiful rainbow trout one more time,* she thought as she dried her eyes and then looked into the river. To her great surprise, there he was, swimming at the surface just in front of her!

She froze in disbelief. The fish circled a few times and then dove into the deep water and returned! Charlie's heart swelled as the rainbow trout looked up at her and she looked back at him. "I knew you would be happy in the river," she told him. The rainbow trout lingered at the surface for a short time and then swam down into the deep, running river.

A large smile spread over her face as she stood up. She picked up her empty bucket and skipped all the way home.

Scavenger Hunt

Can you help Charlie find all her friends?
(Not including the front and back cover)

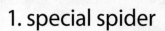

1. special spider

6. green grasshoppers

2. funny frogs

7. lovely ladybugs

3. darling dragonflies

4. wild water skippers

8. beautiful birds

9. brilliant butterflies

5. cute caterpillars

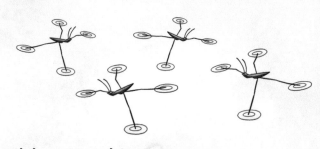

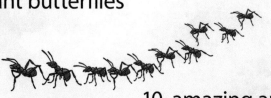
10. amazing ants

Archway Publishing books may be ordered through booksellers or by contacting:

Archway Publishing
1663 Liberty Drive
Bloomington, IN 47403
www.archwaypublishing.com
844-669-3957

ISBN: 978-1-6657-0632-2 (sc)
ISBN: 978-1-6657-0633-9 (hc)
ISBN: 978-1-6657-0634-6 (e)

Print information available on the last page.

Archway Publishing rev. date: 7/1/2021

Printed in the United States
by Baker & Taylor Publisher Services